Editor-in-Chief and Founder:
Lyndon H. LaRouche, Jr.
Editorial Board: *Lyndon H. LaRouche, Jr. , Helga Zepp-LaRouche, Robert Ingraham, Tony Papert, Gerald Rose, Dennis Small, Jeffrey Steinberg, William Wertz*
Co-Editors: *Robert Ingraham, Tony Papert*
Managing Editor: *Nancy Spannaus*
Technology: *Marsha Freeman*
Books: *Katherine Notley*
Ebooks: *Richard Burden*
Graphics: *Alan Yue*
Photos: *Stuart Lewis*
Circulation Manager: *Stanley Ezrol*

INTELLIGENCE DIRECTORS
Counterintelligence: *Jeffrey Steinberg, Michele Steinberg*
Economics: *John Hoefle, Marcia Merry Baker, Paul Gallagher*
History: *Anton Chaitkin*
Ibero-America: *Dennis Small*
Russia and Eastern Europe: *Rachel Douglas*
United States: *Debra Freeman*

INTERNATIONAL BUREAUS
Bogotá: *Miriam Redondo*
Berlin: *Rainer Apel*
Copenhagen: *Tom Gillesberg*
Houston: *Harley Schlanger*
Lima: *Sara Madueño*
Melbourne: *Robert Barwick*
Mexico City: *Gerardo Castilleja Chávez*
New Delhi: *Ramtanu Maitra*
Paris: *Christine Bierre*
Stockholm: *Ulf Sandmark*
United Nations, N.Y.C.: *Leni Rubinstein*
Washington, D.C.: *William Jones*
Wiesbaden: *Göran Haglund*

ON THE WEB
e-mail: eirns@larouchepub.com
www.larouchepub.com
www.executiveintelligencereview.com
www.larouchepub.com/eiw
Webmaster: *John Sigerson*
Assistant Webmaster: *George Hollis*
Editor, Arabic-language edition: *Hussein Askary*

EIR (ISSN 0273-6314) *is published weekly (50 issues), by EIR News Service, Inc., P.O. Box 17390, Washington, D.C. 20041-0390. (703) 777-9451 ext. 415*

European Headquarters: E.I.R. GmbH, Postfach Bahnstrasse 9a, D-65205, Wiesbaden, Germany
Tel: 49-611-73650
Homepage: http://www.eirna.com
e-mail: eirna@eirna.com
Director: Georg Neudecker

Montreal, Canada: 514-461-1557

Denmark: EIR - Danmark, Sankt Knuds Vej 11, basement left, DK-1903 Frederiksberg, Denmark. Tel.: +45 35 43 60 40, Fax: +45 35 43 87 57. e-mail: eirdk@hotmail.com.

Mexico City: EIR, Sor Juana Inés de la Cruz 242-2 Col. Agricultura C.P. 11360 Delegación M. Hidalgo, México D.F. Tel. (5525) 5318-2301 eirmexico@gmail.com

Canada Post Publication Sales Agreement #40683579

Postmaster: Send all address changes to *EIR*, P.O. Box 17390, Washington, D.C. 20041-0390.

Signed articles in *EIR* represent the views of the authors, and not necessarily those of the Editorial Board.

I0407898

Creating Man's Future

Good Grounds for Optimism: A New Paradigm in 2017!

by Helga Zepp-LaRouche, chairwoman of the German Civil Rights Solidarity Movement party (BüSo)

This is Helga Zepp-LaRouche's lead article for the New Year's issue of Neue Solidarität. *Although it is most immediately addressed to a German audience, the message is universal.*

Dec. 31—There is good news: Although Germany is still largely the Valley of the Clueless—thanks to its lock-step mainstream media and the mediocrity of its politicians—our well-informed contemporaries have become aware that over the coming year, a multitude of good tendencies will sweep into Europe, and even into Germany. During 2017 it will become obvious that the strategic reorientation of the greater part of our planet will be determined by the dynamic of the New Silk Road. As a result, the focus will be on an economic new world economic order for the common weal and the conquest of underdevelopment, and not the speculators' profit maximization.

In the course of 2017, it will become clear to the still politically-correct denizens of the Washington Consensus and the EU bureaucracy, the ignorant cadre of the Conservative Revolution, and even many non-political people, that the larger part of humankind has been on the road of creating conditions on Earth *worthy* of humanity for all people for a long time—explicitly as a community for a common destiny of mankind.

In the new year, China will hold two major summits, at which the theme will be the consolidation of the New Silk Road initiative, and where the outstanding attractiveness of the new economic model of win-win cooperation—which has long since become the magnet of

world development—will become clear. Already this global development perspective is the largest infrastructure program in the history of the world, one in which more than 100 nations and international organizations participate, which already affects 4.4 billion people and, for the first time in at least 50 years, presents a realistic hope that the problems of hunger, poverty, treatable diseases, and the denial of education can be conquered once and for all.

In the Middle East, President Putin has brilliantly turned the situation around through Russia's military intervention in Syria: The seemingly endless sequence of wars built upon lies since September 11th, 2001, and the support of rebels speciously called "moderate"—who were given weapons for the murder of segments of the ethnic populations in the Middle East, or for terrorist acts in Europe—were interrupted and put on a good track for termination. At the upcoming meeting in Astana, Kazakhstan at the beginning of 2017, it will be clear that opposition groups in Syria are involved in the reconstruction process, and that the major nations of the region such as Russia, China, India, Iran, and Egypt—and perhaps even former supporters of ISIS and Al-Nusra—can be integrated into a construction plan for all of Southwest Asia. Thus the program to extend the New Silk Road to the Middle East, which the Schiller Institute has been developing since 2012, can be realized in 2017.

It is true that the remaining three short weeks of Obama's administration still represent a threat of further diplomatic "hand grenades," as Obama's expulsion of

人民网
eb.people.cn

Friday, Dec 30, 2016   Search ▾   Archive ▾   Chinese ▾

Home Opinions Business Military World Society Culture Travel Science Sports Special Coverage Photo Video

English >>

Op-Ed: Fixing America will require Trump to be bold, and work with China

By Curtis Stone (People's Daily Online)   15:03, December 30, 2016

President-elect Donald Trump, pictured in a China People's Daily *Online op-ed.*

35 Russian diplomats from the United States has demonstrated. But Putin's reaction, namely, to forego retaliation on the same level and instead to invite the children of U.S. diplomats to the Kremlin for Christmas celebrations, clearly shows who has the upper hand. The savvy Judo Black Belt Putin is clearly superior to the modern-day Nero Obama. Xi Jinping and Putin, who both denounce the moral decadence of the West, and instead promote the moral improvement of their peoples, are morally and practically superior to such people as British front-man George Soros and Obama by orders of magnitude, who with their campaign for the legalization of drugs increase the death rate of the population.

Both President-elect Trump and Moscow have sent many encouraging signals that they have the firm intention to establish relations between the two nations on the basis of productive cooperation. And there is hope that even German Defense Minister Ms. Ursula von der Leyen will conclude that cooperation between the United States and Russia—which in turn is strategically closely linked to China—is the prerequisite for solving most of the problems in this world.

Trump has promised to invest one trillion dollars into the modernization of U.S. infrastructure, and to make it the most modern in the world. That will not

happen without a massive increase of the productivity of the American workforce. The Chinese newspaper *People's Daily* has reacted with an offer under the headline, "Fixing America will require Trump to be bold, and work with China." The article quotes from Trump's book, *Great Again*: "You go to countries like China... and you look at their train systems and their public transport. It's so much better. We're like a third-world country." The article continues self-confidently, "China is leading the world in infrastructure investment and engineering. China's [just completed] Beipan River bridge, which connects Guizhou and Yunnan provinces, is a 4,400-feet-long cable-stayed suspension bridge that hangs 1,854 feet in the sky. That is equivalent to 200 stories, roughly the height of four Trump Towers..."

Trump wants to invest a trillion dollars in infrastructure and create jobs for the population, while China can help with the financing and has substantial knowledge concerning infrastructure. This would help to bring some of the American investments in China back into the United States for America's benefit, and to strengthen bilateral ties. Thus the program which the Schiller Institute has proposed since 2014 for U.S. cooperation with China's New Silk Road, can quickly be put on the agenda. Madam Fu Ying, the chairwoman of the Foreign Affairs Committee of China's legislature, recently presented just this perspective in a speech in New York.

If Republican presidential candidate François Fillon wins the French elections in May as expected, then France will commit itself to ending the European sanctions against Russia. The Austrian government, which will take over the chairmanship of the Organization for Security and Cooperation in Europe (OSCE) in January, has announced the same thing, and a restarting of relations with Russia will also be a theme of this year's Davos World Economic Forum, according to its managing director Philipp Rösler. If German Chancellor Angela Merkel sticks to the prolongation of the sanctions which she had cooked up at her Nov. 18 mini-summit with the defeated Obama, it will get pretty lonely around her.

In view of these tectonic changes in the strategic constellation to be expected in 2017, and further imponderables which could arise, among other things,

A high-speed railway bridge connecting Shanghai and Kunming in the mountainous province of Guizhou.

from the trans-Atlantic banking crisis—triggered by Italy, Deutsche Bank, or another of the thousand mines in the financial system—it is more than questionable whether the EU will continue to exist in its present form, and whether Merkel can win the elections in September. The *BüSo* will participate in these elections with the only program which presents a real answer to the refugee crisis: Germany must participate together with Russia, China, India, Japan, and perhaps with the United States, in large-scale reconstruction programs for the Near and Middle East and for Africa. We have presented concrete plans for this in the study, *The New Silk Road Becomes the World Land-Bridge*, which are already being taken up in several countries as the planning basis for a policy of reconstruction of Southwest Asia and the African continent.

Mrs. Merkel has an obvious recipe for winning the elections: all she need do is make this development per-

spective of the *BüSo* her own. She has demonstrated several times in the past that she is able to make sharp turns, even if usually in a negative direction, as in her un-thought out "energy transition"—the abandonment of nuclear energy—or in her about-face in the refugee crisis, from "We can manage it" ("*Wir schaffen das*"), to support for detention centers for refugees and deployment of EU special "Frontex" border-guards. She has already said that Africa will be an important theme in the next G-20 summit in Hamburg in July. For a genuine change of direction, she would have to eliminate the British influence in her government, which has become blatantly predominant recently. Whether she is capable of this, will be seen in the further careers (or not) of her Anglophile advisers Hans Joachim Schellnhuber and Christoph Heusgen.

In any case, 2017 will be the year in which many aspects of the *BüSo*'s policy will be implemented!

EIR Contents

www.larouchepub.com Volume 44, Number 1, January 6, 2017

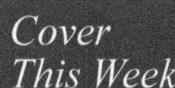

I. New Paradigm in Process of Becoming

Hands Across the Oceans

by Dennis Speed

Jan. 2—The Schiller Institute's New York Community Chorus on December 30 paid its respects to the nation and people of Russia on the occasion of the sudden, tragic death of 64 members of Russia's famed Alexandrov Choir Ensemble in a plane crash on Christmas Day, December 25. Twelve members of the Schiller chorus visited the Russian Consulate in New York City to deliver an official message from Schiller Institute founder Helga Zepp-LaRouche. This sung and written message was presented to the Consulate by Diane Sare, the founder and the conductor of the chorus.

The chorus performed a selection from J.S. Bach's "Wachet Auf," cantata BWV 140, and then sang the Russian national anthem, composed by the Russian choir's founder, Alexander Vasilyevich Alexandrov.

Alexandrov formed what is officially called the "A.V. Alexandrov Academic Ensemble of Song and Dance of the Russian Army" in 1926.

That choir had been on its way to Syria to sing for those engaged in the victorious battle against terrorism in Syria, just concluded in the city of Aleppo by joint Syrian and Russian military forces, including a successful cease-fire. They were to take part in New Year's and Christmas celebrations. (Christmas in the Orthodox confession falls on January 7.)

Ninety-two people in total perished, including the famous "Mother Theresa of Russia," Dr. Liza Galinka, as well as other artists, passengers and crew.

In the statement, which appears in a complete form immediately below in this issue of *EIR*, Zepp-LaRouche stated:

youtube/DjukiNew1957

The Alexandrov Academic Song and Dance Ensemble of the Russian Army, performing at the Tchaikovsky Concert Hall.

The Alexandrov Ensemble has been an expression of the highest moral values of Russia and, like Classical choral singing in general, speaks to the soul and the creative potential of the audience. It is therefore extremely important that Russian Defense Minister Sergei Shoigu announced that he is initiating auditions to find the best talents to fully restore the ensemble.

The training of the singing voice is important for everyone, since a well-placed voice can express the creative intention of the composer and directly speak to the same creative faculty in the audience. It represents, therefore, an irreplaceable element of the harmonious development of the character.

Schiller Institute

Twelve Schiller Institute chorus members being greeted by an official of the Russian Consulate in New York City.

I would therefore like to share with you the idea that, in addition to rebuilding the Alexandrov Ensemble, thousands of Alexandrov choruses could be established in schools all over Russia to honor the heroic contribution of Russia in the liberation of Syria and, at the same time, broaden the uplifting effect of choral singing to the young generation.

The New York City Police Department, represented by Lt. Tony Giorgio, founder and head of the New York City Police Band, was one of the first institutions in the world to mourn the loss. Giorgio was personally very familiar with the ensemble. "Giorgio recalled how the famed Red Army Choir teamed up with the NYPD Band to sing 'God Bless America' at the Quebec City Military Tattoo in 2011, a decade after the 2001 terrorist attacks that struck on New York and Washington, D.C.," recounted *RT Online*:

As the choir sang, Giorgio accepted a single white flower in memory of the lives lost on 9/11. Soloist Grigory Osipov, who led the Quebec performance, was among those who perished in the Tu-154 crash.

Within 24 hours of its being posted on various social media outlets, the Schiller performance had been viewed over a quarter-million times, primarily in Russia and Europe. As of this writing 450,000 persons have viewed it, and there were thousands of comments, the vast majority of which were not only positive, but in one way or another directly referenced the spirit of brotherhood that Schiller's poem "Ode To Joy" also expresses, itself the embodiment of the Institute's universal cultural mission.

• You sang fantastically, thank you. I always knew that ordinary Americans were normal people and not spiteful.

• Thank you! This is the best thing that could be done… This is what real, honest people with a heart and soul are capable of!

• Actions like this reveal the greatness and culture of a nation… Thanks to the performers!

• This, too, will be blamed on Russian hackers.

• This is how understanding between peoples begins, which gives rise to friendship.

• The ordinary people in any country are brothers to each other, and it's a pity when mercenary politicians promote quarrels among them. Thank you, Americans!

• How are our rulers going to rob us, if we live together in peace? That is their nightmare.

• St. George ribbons. Americans with St. George

Schiller Institute

Twelve members of the New York Schiller Institute chorus pay its respects in song, and with a message from the founder of the Schiller Institutes, Helga Zepp-LaRouche, after the tragic death of 64 members of the Russian Alexandrov Choir Ensemble.

weighs all the negatives of relations between our countries in recent times.

• So there are at least 12 singing, sane citizens in America! Not everybody is a Psaki! That is reason to be happy! As for our anthem, it really is pretty cool. During sports broadcasts [the poster is evidently a cameraman] I get to hear it alongside the anthems of other countries. It's majestic.

• Western media: Putin forces Americans to sing anthem at the point of a Kalashnikov! Seriously, though,

ribbons. What are the Ukrainians to make of that?...

• Thank you, guys! Moved to tears... One more confirmation that the American people do not embrace the abominations committed by the American elites. Thank you, American people! Let's be friends, not enemies!

• Russians value and remember a display of humanity like this. You have done something great, and worthy of the great American nation, and you did it in the best way. Thank you!

• It had seemed to me that all such actions were nothing but flashmobs and other insincere movements, done for self-advertisement!! But I see that things only seemed like that! The simple truths, which everybody is bored with—mercy, sympathy, and honor—*are alive!* And in a place where we had lost hope of seeing them! That is so good! Thank you!

• Brilliant! The Schiller Institute Chorus members sing wonderfully! Beautifully and from the heart! What's more, they managed to inject more profound meaning into the words of the Russian anthem, as if opening it up "from the inside."

• In my opinion, this action by people of art out-

thank you guys!

The Schiller Institute's action was the exact opposite of that taken in the creation of the CIA's Congress for Cultural Freedom against the then-Soviet Union at the Waldorf Astoria Hotel in 1949. That "cultural Cold War" is now being brought to an end. The departure of the Obama Administration, itself a sort of "CCF product," which thought it appropriate to banish 35 Russian diplomats in the same week as the tragedy occurred, is none too soon.

The avowed intent of the incoming Trump Administration to seek the path of cooperation with Russia, particularly in the fight against terrorism, and with China and other nations in joint, mutual economic development, must be informed by higher cultural standards than those unfortunately presented to the world up until the moment of Obama's removal from the Presidency—a removal still better done prior to January 20, Inauguration Day.

Why wait? Such actions as the Schiller New York Community Chorus initiated toward the Russian people are the moral equivalent of removing Obama from office now, such that the spirit, if not the letter of an "American New Deal for the world," might be foreseen, though not simply willed into being. The "new world cultural bridge" that can now be built, need not wait for another moment. The overture may, indeed should, come in a well-composed musical piece, before the opening of the first act.

HELGA ZEPP-LAROUCHE

Message of Condolence To the Alexandrov Ensemble And the People of Russia

Dec. 30—In the name of the International Schiller Institute, I wish to express our deep condolences for the tragic loss of the 92 human beings who died in the plane crash on their way to Syria, most of whom were members of the Alexandrov Ensemble. This accident is all the more a cause for sadness, as the music and patriotic spirit characteristic of the members of the Alexandrov Ensemble would have brought a message of hope to the people of Syria. This is a people victimized by more than five years of the criminal policies of regime change and treated as the pawns in a geopolitical game in complete violation of their nation's sovereignty.

The Alexandrov Ensemble has been an expression of the highest moral values of Russia and, like Classical choral singing in general, speaks to the soul and the creative potential of its audience. It is therefore extremely important that Russian Defense Minister Sergei Shoigu has announced that he is initiating auditions to find the best talents to fully restore the ensemble.

The training of the singing voice is important for everyone, since a well-placed voice can express the creative intention of the composer and directly speak to the same creative faculty in the audience. It represents, therefore, an irreplaceable element of the harmonious development of the character.

I would therefore like to share with you the idea that, in addition to rebuilding the Alexandrov Ensem-

ble, thousands of Alexandrov choruses could be established in schools all over Russia to honor the heroic contribution of Russia in the liberation of Syria and, at the same time, to broaden the uplifting effect of choral singing on the younger generation.

A New Paradigm is now coming into being, as exemplified by the integration of the Eurasian Economic Union and the New Silk Road Initiative, establishing a completely new kind of relations among nations. We need a dialogue of the best traditions of each culture for this New Paradigm to grow into a new era of civilization: Knowledge of the best of another culture will lead to a love for it, and will thereby supersede xenophobia and hatred with more noble emotions. In this new era, geopolitics will be overcome forever, and dedication to the common aims of mankind will establish a higher level of reason. It is a consolation for all of us, that the tragic death of the victims of this plane crash will contribute with their immortality to the building of that better world.

Helga Zepp-LaRouche
Chairwoman, International Schiller
Institute

This message was received at the Russian Consulate in New York on the afternoon of Dec. 30, and was also sent on request to the Russian news agency TASS.

The New Paradigm Requires U.S.-China Cooperation

by Kesha Rogers

Jan. 1—China continues to offer an outstretched hand of cooperation to the United States, as it moves ahead as a world leader in economic and scientific development. On Nov. 12, 2014, Chinese President Xi Jinping made the following offer of cooperation to President Obama and the United States, during a joint press conference of the two presidents in the Great Hall of the Peoples, in Beijing:

> Ladies and gentlemen, friends, China is ready to work with the United States to make efforts in a number of priority areas and putting into effect such principles as non-confrontation, non-conflict, mutual respect, and win-win cooperation. And with unwavering spirit and unremitting efforts, we will promote new progress in building a new type model of major-country relations between the two countries so as to bring greater benefits to our two peoples and two countries.

Although Obama refused this offer outright, China has not taken it off the table. The need for cooperation has only increased, and was put forth in a new way to the Trump Presidency on Dec. 6. The Trump Presidency has already indicated an openness to this offer.

How To 'Make America Great Again'

But cooperation is not enough. The new, worldwide win-win paradigm, initiated by China, requires that America become great again, as is made clear by my South African colleague, R.P. Tsokolibane,

in his letter of New Year's greetings to President-elect Trump (see page 33 of this issue).

With the election of Trump, a new opening has presented itself: The destructive Bush-Obama era—of economic collapse and dismantling of our productive labor force—can end. The Trump Presidency intends to put an end to it, and to "make America great again." That, however, will require an entirely new approach to economics and international relations.

The United States must once again take direction from the leadership of our first Treasury Secretary, Alexander Hamilton, and implement a massive program for rebuilding the nation, just as Franklin Roosevelt did in the Great Depression. Since the death of Franklin Roosevelt and the abandonment of the principle of physical economic development, the United States'

White House photo

President Xi Jinping in Beijing, Nov. 12, 2014

labor force has declined to an abysmal state, as its skills were increasingly held in contempt. Lyndon LaRouche, who stands on the shoulders of Hamilton and Roosevelt, has specified Four New Laws for immediate enactment as the basis for a U.S. recovery, a new economic orientation for our future, and successful international cooperation.

LaRouche's four measures—reinstate Roosevelt's Glass-Steagall Act to protect capital from speculation, return to a Hamiltonian national bank, create and earmark federal credit for productive work, and launch a crash program for nuclear fusion power—must be seen as facets of a single principle, a commitment to the self-development of the human species.

China National Space Administration

China's Chang'e-5 mission, to be launched Oct. 23, 2017, will perform the first-ever landing on the lunar far side. It will collect samples and return them to Earth.

For Cooperation, Start from the Top

America's return to greatness must include international cooperation in space exploration and development—as a science-driver for the world economy. Space exploration and development is also the arena in which the spirit of working toward the common aims of mankind is most readily elicited.

Cooperation with China in space is a leading agenda item that the Trump Presidency must bring fully to life, especially because, as the United States' space program has been destructively cut back, step by step, under Bush and Obama, China's program has leapt ahead.

For its part, China continues to demonstrate its increased commitment to international cooperation and peaceful development among nations in space, as also on Earth.

In China's white paper on its space activities in 2016, released Dec. 28, China puts great emphasis on the need for peaceful development and international cooperation, and identifies the areas in which such cooperation already exists.

In the paper's statement of China's vision, it says in part,

> To build China into a space power in all respects, with the capabilities to make innovations independently, to make scientific discovery and research at the cutting edge, to promote strong and sustained economic and social development, to effectively and reliably guarantee national secu-

rity, to exercise sound and efficient governance, and to carry out mutually beneficial international exchanges and cooperation. (Section I.2)

Under "International Exchanges and Cooperation," it states,

> The Chinese government holds that all countries in the world have equal rights to peacefully explore, develop, and utilize outer space and its celestial bodies, and that all countries' outer space activities should be beneficial to their economic development and social progress, and to the peace, security, survival, and development of mankind. (Section V)

The paper notes that China has signed 43 space cooperation agreements or memoranda of understanding with 29 countries, space agencies, and international organizations since 2011.

In a section on peaceful development in space, it says:

> China always adheres to the principle of the use of outer space for peaceful purposes, and opposes the weaponization of, or an arms race in outer space. The country develops and utilizes space resources in a prudent manner, takes effec-

Trump: "We're like a third-world country." This bridge over the Mississippi River in Minneapolis, Minn., collapsed on Aug. 14, 2007.

tion of the Moon. (Section III.4)

U.S.-China cooperation in space is thus of importance for *global economic development*, in light of LaRouche's Four Laws, and of what China has accomplished in space already. The Trump Presidency must understand its importance and come to grips with its potential.

And on Earth

The benefits of cooperation in building terrestrial infrastructure—another key aspect of China's standing offer to the United States—were outlined in a Dec. 30 op-ed in *People's Daily* online, titled, "Fixing America Will Require Trump to be Bold, and Work with China." It says in part:

> In U.S. President-elect Donald Trump's book, *Great Again*, he said, "You go to countries like China … and you look at their train systems and their public transport. It's so much better. We're like a third-world country." Despite his tough talk, Trump admires China for its GDP growth and for its infrastructure investment and engineering. He sees that, while America is aging and falling behind in certain areas, China is growing and moving forward. The U.S. can learn from China on infrastructure building, and benefit from its successes.

China's Belt and Road Initiative has plunged ahead in providing economic development at home, throughout Asia, and around the world.

The op-ed accurately poses the challenge facing the new Presidency and once again states clearly that cooperation with China is pertinent:

> America may be the contemporary example on building a great country, but China is the contemporary example on rebuilding a great country. The two massive bridges in Guizhou are a tiny

tive measures to protect the space environment to ensure a peaceful and clean outer space, and guarantee that its space activities benefit the whole of mankind. (Section I.3)

The most notable of the "Major Tasks for the Next Five Years" outlined in the white paper is its report on deep-space exploration. China will—

> fulfill the three strategic steps of "orbiting, landing, and returning" for the lunar exploration project by launching the Chang'e-5 lunar probe by the end of 2017 and realizing a regional soft landing, sampling, and return. We will launch the Chang'e-4 lunar probe around 2018 to achieve mankind's first soft landing on the far side of the Moon, and conduct *in situ* and roving detection and relay communications at Earth-Moon L2 point [Lagrange Point 2].

> Through the lunar exploration project, topographic and geological surveys will be implemented and laboratory research conducted on lunar samples; geological survey and research as well as low-frequency radio astronomy observation and research will be carried out targeting the landing area on the far side of the Moon for a better understanding of the formation and evolu-

example of China's strength in infrastructure investment and engineering. No other country in the world has lifted more than double the size of America's entire population out of poverty in such a short period of time. Since then, China has opened the Asian Infrastructure Investment Bank, and is building the Silk Road Economic Belt and the 21st Century Maritime Silk Road. These are massive cooperation projects, and the hallmark of modern-day China.

China News Service/Pan Xianyang

World's highest bridge, the Beipan River expressway bridge—part of a highway linking the cities of Hangzhou and Ruili—opened Dec. 29, 2016.

Meanwhile, America cannot even realize high-speed rail after years and years of planning. Rather than bash China, perhaps America should learn from and work with China.

The op-ed ends with a reference to Trump's intended $1 trillion of infrastructure upgrades in America to rebuild the nation and put the people back to work. These projects are to be carried out over the next 10 years. China has been spending a trillion dollars *per year* for the past decade! Again, Lyndon LaRouche has laid out the measures to be taken in the United States for a rapid recovery program and restoring our labor force. Take a lesson from Alexander Hamilton and China today! It is the inalienable right of mankind to develop.

The U.S. in the New World Economy

A rapid recovery program in the United States will require U.S. participation in a new system of cooperative relations among nations. Indeed, the world *is* now moving rapidly toward a new global paradigm of economic development. The United States must take measures to join in. According to LaRouche, "America, Russia, and China must join hands for security and prosperity."

For many years, LaRouche and his wife Helga Zepp-LaRouche have developed strategies for international cooperation and development as the only possible means for defeating a failed—but still dangerous—unipolar system of globalization and free trade, which has dominated the planet since the collapse of the Soviet Union. Now, with the leadership that has emerged in Russia and China most notably, the potential for a new paradigm and an economic renaissance for mankind is on the rise.

How do we in the United States develop a new economic platform? How will we contribute to the increase in the level of productivity of the world economy from the standpoint of the common aims of mankind?

In reflecting on how the United States can and must be integrated into the rapidly advancing global alliance, Helga Zepp-LaRouche developed the following thought: "If you want to have cooperation among countries and a new set of relations, then you must look for the strength of one country economically, scientifically … look for the strength in one country to build up the other … Where are the strengths of each economy to upgrade the productivity of the other?"

These are questions that must be central for the incoming Trump administration. The solutions posed by Lyndon LaRouche always come back to the principle of advancing the productive powers—the cognitive and creative powers—of our labor force, just as we witnessed during the Presidency of Franklin Roosevelt and through the Apollo Program under President Kennedy.

As Lyndon LaRouche recently declared, "Get the United States cranked up to see a clear vision, as was done with FDR in 1930s."

A LESSON FROM FDR

Uplifting the People

by Robert Ingraham and Theodore Andromidas

I. Introduction

Jan. 2—As the sixteen-year nightmare of George W. Bush and Barack Obama draws to a close, we find America in a great crisis, confronted with a series of choices as to what the nation's new direction will be in the months ahead. Our major banking and financial institutions are all insolvent; our industry and manufacturing have been plundered and shuttered; our nation is ravaged by an out-of-control drug epidemic; and America's once great and proud tradition of leadership in science and technology has all but vanished, with the deliberate abandonment of any national commitment to either the development of Fusion Energy or an aggressive Space Program.

Obviously, much can be said in regard to urgently-needed actions. These would include a major change in foreign policy, including friendly overtures to both Russia and China, and a willingness on the part of the United States to join in the new paradigm of global economic development. Such necessary actions also includes the passage of Glass-Steagall legislation and the implementation of a Hamiltonian credit policy to rebuild America's physical economy.

At the same time, however, even as the structures and components of our nation have been dismantled and damaged almost beyond repair, an even greater crisis exists as to the moral and intellectual carnage that has been wreaked on the minds and souls of the American people. We are dealing today with a severely damaged population, a population which has been reduced to the level of effective moral, economic and cultural slavery. The chains that have been imposed over the last sixteen years will not be easy to break. And the greatest of all the harm that has been inflicted has been that which has been done to the youth of America.

This current article will deal, extensively, with measures that were taken by President Franklin Roosevelt. It is not, however, intended to be an "history" article, something which tells an interesting or inspiring story. We can learn from the past—yet, our focus is the crisis of today and the initiatives which must be taken now to move America toward rapid and sustainable improvement.

II. Lyndon LaRouche Speaks

On Tuesday, Dec. 27, 2016, during a conference call with associates, Lyndon LaRouche had the following to say, regarding the matters with which we are here concerned,

TheGadgetGuy1/youtube

Detroit 2016: an abandoned auto plant.

You've got to get the people back into understanding what is available to them. We've got to break the ice on slavery, on various kinds and degrees of slavery, inside the United States. And the ruin of our education system, all these kinds of things. These things have to be rebuilt. Because it is those kinds of things which, when done properly, will cause the leading of the recovery of the United States population...

Most of the people of the United States have been brainwashed. And I do mean, literally, brainwashed. And that's the thing you've got to correct. You've got to bring people who are actually ignorant, not just ignorant of particular things but ignorant in their behavior towards society in general. And if we want to win this thing, win a recovery of the U.S. economy, you've got to do that.

I think we have the latent option, in the United States, on this thing. I think we can probably get that back, again, and can push away the kind of thing that destroyed the financial system, the U.S. financial system, when President Franklin Roosevelt was crushed. It was that simple. And this is what you've got to have, is the leadership which goes like Franklin Roosevelt's campaigns; goes to the issues of what is necessary to instruct people to recognize the things that will make them better in terms of their behavior in society.

You have to really educate people, by using the kinds of tools of education which make them creative. That used to happen in the United States, that used to happen. And then it went down, when Franklin Roosevelt dropped out. But now we've seen everything, all the dirty business in the United States is still there and it has to be removed. In other words all these things, of the people who were opposed to Franklin Roosevelt, that has to be removed and a vision of what Franklin Roosevelt had accomplished, in a decade, particularly, that's what has to be created, and based on.

Thus, our task is defined, and the direction toward a solution is supplied by Mr. LaRouche. What is left to us is: first, to accept both the analysis and challenge as defined by LaRouche, without any short-cuts or quick-results schemes; and second, to organize and fight for this perspective and policy orientation.

III. Our Current Situation

As of Jan. 1, 2017 there are approximately thirty-two million Americans between the ages of eighteen and twenty-four. If one takes a larger segment, there are almost eighty million Americans between the ages of seventeen and thirty-four. In other words, the "youth population" of America is equal in size to the total population of Germany or Iran. All of these youth have spent the majority, if not the near entirety of their lives under the immoral and inhuman policies of Bush and Obama.

What is the culture of this "youth nation"? They possess no sense of purpose for their lives, beyond mere personal desires; no sense of mission; no positive national identity; no sense of what it means to be productive; an almost complete lack of real labor skills, among all but a small minority; an almost total lack of classical culture; and a crippling inability to concentrate and work through difficult intellectual problems over a sustained time-period. Many small businesses and corporations describe the majority of American youth as "unemployable."

According to a report issued by the Economic Policy Institute in 2016, actual youth unemployment,[1] for high school graduates, stands at 33.8 percent for whites, 51.3 percent for blacks and 36.1 percent for Hispanics. It is far worse for those who have not completed high school, and even for college graduates, the national average is still over 20 percent.

At the same time, it is now reported by the Centers for Disease Control that one out of fifteen Americans is now addicted to heroin or some other opioid. That's 20 million Americans who are addicted. And these figures do not include consumption of methamphetamines, hallucinogens, ecstasy, or other "designer" drugs. Additionally, recent studies from states which have legalized marijuana indicate a significant jump in overall drug usage since legalization has taken effect. The impairment of cognitive functioning that has resulted from this saturation-level drug usage is beyond dispute.

Most readers have probably heard the term "Hoovervilles" used to describe the decrepit shanty-towns erected by the homeless during the 1920s and 1930s.

---

1. That is, figures which reflect the combined total of the "official" unemployment rate, those whom the government omits as "not in the labor force," and those who are severely and unwillingly underemployed, many employed for only a few hours a week at minimum wage jobs.

They are back, but today's "Obamavilles" are much worse than their depression-era predecessors. On your computer, go to Google and type in the phrase, "Tent City" (or "Homeless Encampment") United States 2016. Look at the images. There are now thousands, perhaps tens of thousands, of such "camps" across the country. They are in every one of the fifty states. The majority of the residents are under thirty-five years old. Malnutrition, drug usage, disease and crime are rampant. This is now the reality—the day-to-day life—for those inhabiting these camps.

EIRNS/Michael Steger

A tent city in Ontario, Calif.

What we are facing today not simply an "economic" crisis. It is the very soul of America which is imperiled. Wake up! The danger today is actually far greater than during Roosevelt's lifetime. The damage is greater. When Roosevelt took office in 1933, the factories had only been shut down for three or four or five years. Now, it has been longer than an entire generation. Young people today do not even possess the memory of a time when America had a productive economy. The generation which put a man on the Moon is dead or dying, and their skills are dying with them.

At the same time, America has been at war for fifteen years, brutal, evil wars which are a disgrace to America's founding intention. If you are now eighteen years old, those wars began when you were two or three years old, perhaps only recently out of diapers. You have known nothing else your entire life. For the last eight years a man has occupied the White House who takes glee in murdering people each week, through drone attacks and other

East Liverpool, Ohio Mobile Upload

Overdosed grandparents passed out in car, with child in back seat.

means. If you are now twenty years old, these government-authorized murders have been going on since you were twelve. How is it possible to comprehend a profound love of one's country, let alone to possess confident optimism in the future, under these conditions?

The drugs have made this crisis far, far worse. As bad as the prohibition-era, jazz-age, speakeasy culture of the 1920s and 30s was, nothing in human history compares to the destruction of the human identity which is being wrought by today's escalating drug usage.

Why focus this article on youth? Aren't all Americans, from all age groups, suffering? Yes, they are, but youth are the future. They can not and must not be abandoned, either morally or from the standpoint of national security. As stated, there are 80 million young adults in America. With them, we rise or fall. It is not an accident that the average age of an enrollee in one of Franklin Roosevelt's CCC camps was twenty. FDR rescued an entire generation, one which otherwise had no future, except perhaps as fodder for a growing fascist movement. This is where the intervention, no matter how difficult, has to be made, and it must be made now.

IV. Franklin Roosevelt's Victory

Lyndon LaRouche has often described the great turning point in human history which took place with the 1890 forced ouster of German Chancellor Bismarck and the 1901 assassination of U.S. President William McKinley.

Homelessness epidemic in the 1930s.

irwinator.com

From 1890 onward, all of Europe as well as the United States began a descent into what can only be described as a "New Dark Age," a process which was dramatically intensified as a result of the destruction and horrors of World War I.

During those 40-plus years, leading into 1933, there was a continual decimation and demoralization of culture both in Europe and America. In science, in the classical arts, in economics, the hard-fought progress which had been achieved during the eighteenth and nineteenth centuries was rolled back. By 1933, not only were Germany and Italy both governed by fascist regimes, but most of the rest of Europe, most emphatically Britain and France, were dominated by a pessimistic fascist culture. The same process also occurred in the United States, typified by the major revival of the Ku Klux Klan in the 1920s.

Then came Franklin Roosevelt. Beginning in March of 1933, FDR—like a lightning bolt—took the United States in an entirely different direction.

President Franklin Roosevelt, ca. 1941.

http://nddaily.blogspot.com

He returned the United States to the intention of the Constitution and the Declaration of Independence. Despite massive opposition from London and Wall Street, he turned America on a dime. In economics, education, science and the arts, he revived and re-created the American Spirit. He, alone,[2] defied the moral and economic degeneration of that era. He, alone, defeated the slide into fascist pessimism. He set out to rescue and uplift the American people. He succeeded. That is the lesson we must learn for the challenge of today.

Creating a Solution

Consider, carefully, what Franklin Roosevelt initiated during his first 100 Days. None of it came from a "recipe book." All of it was new. Things were done, experiments in policy were carried out, none of which had been done before, by anyone, at any previous time in human history. Solutions could not be copied from past events; creative interventions were required. Hovering over every action was a governing principle—to rescue and uplift the population and to rebuild the nation's productive capabilities.

Far too often, when someone says that we need "productive" investment as opposed to "speculative" investment, this is taken to mean that we need more manufacturing. But if thousands of factories are producing designer tee-shirts or video games, does this signify an increase in the nation's productivity? Productivity begins with devel-

---

2. One might add the quite different, even unique, role of the Soviet Union in this period as a second point of opposition to the dark age collapse in Europe.

Works Progress Administration workers.

FDR Library

Norris Dam in Tennessee, part of the Tennessee Valley Authority project.

U.S. National Archives and Records Administration

CCC workers constructing a road, 1933.

National Archives and Records Administration

FERA camps for unemployed women in Arcola, Pennsylvania. "Second Camp" shown here ca. July 1934.

oping the power of the individual human mind. People matter. At the same time that Franklin Roosevelt launched the unprecedented Tennessee Valley Authority (TVA) project in 1933, he also created both the Civilian Conservation Corps (CCC) and the Federal Emergency Relief Administration (FERA), which together rescued seven million unemployed Americans—mostly young—and gave them jobs. Later, he would also create both the Civil Works Administration (CWA) and the Works Progress Administration (WPA), the latter of which employed an additional eight million, three million of whom were hired in its first year of operation.

Roosevelt's priority was to overcome the profound social crisis and human suffering within the nation. A type of "conveyor belt" was established, wherein young Americans, as they were rescued from despair and degradation, entered into an upward process of developing new skills, new talents, and new productive powers. People moved up from unskilled or semi-skilled labor to more sophisticated forms of employment, many joining the larger, more ambitious projects of the Public Works Administration or finding positions within the revived U.S. manufacturing sector. The dynamic was one of upward mobility, aided by the development of new skills and educational opportunities. It is not a fluke, that as World War II approached, the United States Army actively sought out and recruited veterans of the Civilian Conservation Corps and enlisted many of them directly as NCOs (sergeants and corporals) to aid in the development of raw recruits.

Jobs

In March of 1933, the U.S. Congress, at the request of President Roosevelt, created the Civilian Conservation Corps. Six weeks later Congress established the Federal Emergency Relief Administration (FERA). FERA, between 1933 and 1935, created more than twenty million jobs, the equivalent of forty-five million jobs given our larger population today.

Franklin Roosevelt placed Harry Hopkins in charge of FERA, and Hopkins personified FDR's demand for "action, and action now"! In his first two *hours* on the job, Hopkins approved more than $5 million in grants to various states for federal funding for "shovel ready" projects. Later, in November of 1933, the Civil Works Administration (CWA) was created as a subsidiary agency within FERA. This was designed from the beginning as a temporary measure. In its five months of existence, the CWA created four million jobs (the equivalent of nine million today). State governments submitted thousands of requests for aid in funding local projects, and, at one point, Hopkins was approving 100 projects per day.

Many historians have derided these jobs as "make work" or "ditch-digging" jobs, yet two points must be made on this. First, the CWA did not simply dig ditches or rake leaves. It laid twelve million feet of sewer pipe, and built or made substantial improvements to 255,000 miles of roads, 40,000 schools, and nearly 1,000 airports. It also provided considerable white-collar work, employing 50,000 teachers, as well as architects, bookbinders, writers and artists. At the same time, it is urgent to recognize that the CWA's employment of four million otherwise desperate Americans into projects which produced visible, tangible improvements in the condition of the nation, is precisely the means whereby optimism is nurtured. Despair is turned into hope.

A full rendition of all of the accomplishments of the New Deal is not possible here. Let us simply state, that

newdealprogressives.org

President Franklin Roosevelt discussing plans with close assistant Harry Hopkins (left).

under FERA, the CWA, the CCC, and the WPA, more than 14,000 new schools were built (and tens of thousands more repaired or upgraded) and more than 1,000 new public libraries; 12,000 road projects were carried out, and more than 120,000 new buildings, including post offices, courthouses, firehouses and armories, were constructed. Soil conservation, mosquito abatement, flood control and other useful projects were accomplished. These projects were carried out, not only in every state, but in almost all of the cities, towns and villages within the nation. Nearly every community in the United States had a new park, bridge or school constructed by one of these agencies.

In 1935, Roosevelt also established the National Youth Administration (NYA). Under this program, the government made it possible for 1.5 million high school students and 600,000 college students—the age range was from sixteen to twenty-five—to continue their education by providing them with part-time jobs. A key component of the program was job training. Although in recent years such vocational training has been rightfully criticized as a form of "tracking" of poor students into lower wage occupations, it must be understood that in 1933-1937 most of these students had no skills at all, and very little in the way of job prospects. The NYA exposed students to a wide variety of fields, including education, the arts, research and development, manufacturing, agriculture, and construction. As in the case of the CCC, with the outbreak of World War II, many of the NYA "alumni" played a significant role as secondary or even primary leaders in the development of de-

Young men of Company 2314-C, Kane, Pennsylvania, study radio code in a camp.

sources, create future national wealth and prove of moral and spiritual value not only to those of you who are taking part, but to the rest of the country as well… You should emerge from this experience strong and rugged and ready for entrance into the ranks of industry, better equipped than before. Opportunities for employment in work, for which individually you are best suited, are increasing daily, and you should emerge from this experience splendidly equipped for the competitive fields of endeavor which always mark the industrial life of America.

A New Economic Platform

During his first 100 Days, Franklin Roosevelt also established both the Public Works Administration (PWA) and the Tennessee Valley Authority. Space prohibits a lengthy discussion here of either of these two projects.

Let us simply state that the PWA was tasked with responsibility for the building of larger infrastructure projects, many of which produced a powerful effect in improving the economic productivity of the nation. Among the PWA's many accomplishments were the construction of the Grand Coulee Dam, the Bonneville Dam, the Triborough Bridge, the Lincoln Tunnel, La-Guardia Airport, Los Angeles Airport, and the Upper Mississippi River locks and dams. There were hundreds of such projects, including canals, tunnels, bridges, and highways. Like the WPA, the PWA also built scores of new schools, libraries, hospitals, post offices and playgrounds. It was also involved, in partnership with the Rural Electrification Administration, in projects which led to the successful electrification of the entire nation.

Unlike the WPA or the CCC, the PWA operated largely by contracting out projects to private companies. The PWA spent over $6 billion in contracts to private construction firms, and much of the workforce for these projects was more skilled, for example, than the typical CCC recruit. In some respects, the PWA model might serve today as a framework for the involvement of private corporations, such as Caterpillar and Bechtel, in projects such as the Bering Strait tunnel, a national high-speed rail project, and the development of new fresh water capacities.

fense industries and the emergence of the productive capabilities of the war economy.

The Civilian Conservation Corps is of particular relevance for today, because its base for recruitment was entirely composed of unskilled, impoverished and often homeless youth.[3] These were the children of the "Roaring 20s," many of whom grew up in a culture of crime and widespread alcohol and even drug use. It is not much talked about today, but there were more than 300,000 drug addicts in the United States in 1925 (in a total population of 115 million), and many Hollywood movies and "jazz" recordings of that time glorified drug usage, including cocaine, opium and marijuana. The CCC moved millions of youth out of their home towns and into facilities where, in addition to the daily work projects, educational instruction, reading skills, music and art were provided.

In his third Fireside Chat, on July 8, 1933, FDR would report to the American people the successful establishment and the importance of the Civilian Conservation Corps.

> I welcome the opportunity to extend a greeting to the men who constitute the Civilian Conservation Corps… It is my belief that what is being accomplished will conserve our natural re-

---

3. The despair facing American youth at that time was the subject of a number of films, including 1933's *Wild Boys of the Road* by William Wellman.

La Guardia Airport, built in New York City by the WPA in 1939.

PWA projects created a "multiplier effect," and it is estimated that for every worker on a PWA project, two additional workers were employed indirectly in the private sector. During its years of operation, PWA projects consumed roughly half of the concrete and a third of the steel of the entire nation.

As to the Tennessee Valley Authority, in a nutshell, Franklin Roosevelt took an area, including parts of seven states and encompassing an area eighty percent the size of England, and utterly transformed it, utilizing the most advanced industrial, technological and scientific means available at that time. The region in question was the poorest in the nation, with only a small fraction of the residents having access to electricity. Income for many families was below $100 per year, and thirty percent of the population was affected by malaria.

Under the slogan of "electricity for all," more than forty-five dams and hydro-electric projects were built. Additionally, more than twenty coal-fired and natural gas power plants were constructed. Later, after World War II, the TVA would embark on an ambitious project for the construction of nuclear power reactors. A region of the nation, one which encompassed 80,000 square miles, was transformed from the most abject poverty and cultural ignorance, into a driver for a dramatic increase in the economic productivity of the entire nation.

The Measure of Success

Between 1933 and 1937 unemployment was reduced from 22.6 percent to 9.1 percent. By no means was this improvement all due to direct government employment. In May 1935, private sector industrial production was fifty-five percent higher than in May 1933. By 1937, industrial production surpassed pre-1929 levels. The multiplier effect from PWA, TVA and related projects was felt throughout the private manufacturing, agricultural and construction sectors.

At the same time, the profound consequences which flowed from Roosevelt's banking reforms, including most particularly the Glass-Steagall Act, as well as from the initiatives of the Reconstruction Finance Corporation, choked off much of the pre-1933 non-productive speculative investments in the financial sector, while simultaneously establishing a Hamiltonian-type flow of credit into productive, physical investment.

Bear in mind that all of this was accomplished within the context of a global economic depression, of contracting trade and shrinking markets. It was also accomplished over the intense opposition of Wall Street and the City of London, whose intention never wavered from destroying Roosevelt, destroying the New Deal, and plunging the United States into the same downward-spiraling crisis which gripped Europe.

Roosevelt succeeded, but let us again emphasize that his success must not be measured in statistics, let alone in dollar figures. Rather, the actual success is seen in the uplifting and transformation of the people of the nation, in increasing the moral and cognitive powers of those same people. Alexander Hamilton would have recognized this yardstick for success, and it is important that we perceive clearly what it is that must be done today.

V. Developing the Mind

As already stated, in looking at the various construction projects of the WPA, FERA, and the CWA, one is struck by the great number of schools and libraries which were built or modernized. Throughout the New Deal, a stress was placed on the question of literacy.

If one looks at why the American Revolution succeeded and why, for example the French Revolution descended into barbarism, literacy—that which elevates the human mind—is at the very center of the difference. At the time of the American Revolution, literacy rates stood at near 100 percent in the major cities of Boston, New York and Philadelphia, and the American colonies possessed possibly the most literate culture in the world. In *Literacy in Colonial New England*, author Kevin Lockridge used legal records to demonstrate that,

> Among white New England men, about 60 percent of the population was literate between 1650 and 1670, a figure that rose to 85 percent between 1758 and 1762, and to 90 percent between 1787 and 1795.

Comparing this to what later existed in the United States in 1930, we see a shocking decline of literacy, a decline which accelerated dramatically after Ulysses Grant's 1875 Civil Rights Act was declared unconstitutional in 1883. The rate of student enrollment in America's schools in 1930 was almost exactly the same rate of enrollment as in 1830, which itself was a decline from the Revolutionary War period. And, although rates fluctuated, in general, by 1930, only half of all five to eighteen year-olds were enrolled in school. Rates for African-Americans were much lower than for whites.

In the southern states, the situation, even among whites, was far worse. Fewer than five percent of the teachers in this region had college training; more than sixty percent had no definite professional training of any kind. While illiteracy ranged from thirty to forty-five percent of the total population in the southern half of the nation (three times that of other areas of the country), only one southern pupil out of ten who enrolled in school reached the fifth grade, and only one in seventy reached the eighth grade.

National Archives

Violin instruction under the direction of the WPA Federal Music Project in New York City.

This situation would not change until the New Deal. Then the overall enrollment rates for five to eighteen year-olds rose from fifty-one percent in 1930 to seventy-five percent in 1940. The difference in the white and black enrollment rates narrowed from twenty-three points to seven points. Under Franklin Roosevelt, more than 31,000 schools were either built or renovated.

The Arts

In 1935 Franklin Roosevelt created Federal Project Number One, known as "Federal One," for short. This project not only extended economic relief and protection to artists, actors, writers, and musicians, but it also initiated a sweeping, in-depth effort to bring the civilizing benefits of music and classical culture to tens of millions of Americans.

Three years after the establishment of Federal One, Roosevelt wrote to his friend, the journalist Hendrik Willem Van Loon, "I too, have a dream—to show people in the out of the way places, some of whom are not only in small villages but in corners of New York City—something they cannot get from between the covers of books, some real paintings and prints and etchings and some real music."

At the heart of Federal One was the Federal Music Project, and between 1935 and 1938, 275,000 live "performances, programs, and recitals" were given, performed before 147,000,000 people in forty-three states and Washington, D.C. The number of symphony orchestras in the nation rose from nineteen to one hundred fifty-three, with the Federal Music Project directly creating thirty-four new orchestras and aiding in the creation of one hundred more.

The more profound aspect of this effort, however, did not lie simply in the aid it provided to professional musicians, but the ambitious musical education program it initiated. The Federal Music Project provided classes

National Archives

A WPA Federal Music Project production of Macbeth.

in rural areas and urban neighborhoods, providing music education in all public schools. The program recruited and retrained approximately 1,600 music teachers, and the classes over which these teachers presided included hundreds of thousands of students, classes which included both vocal and instrumental instruction.

Thousands of new and used musical instruments, including violins, cellos, flutes and oboes, were purchased and made available, free of charge, to young students in musical programs throughout the nation.

Before the Federal Music Project came into existence, it had been estimated that two-thirds of the 4,000,000 children in the 143,000 rural schools in America were without music instruction in any form. The activities of its music teachers penetrated into the remotest rural communities. These teachers also were leading large classes in the slums and congested areas of the great cities. Classical music became the "people's music," available to urban and rural areas alike, to the wealthy and the poor.

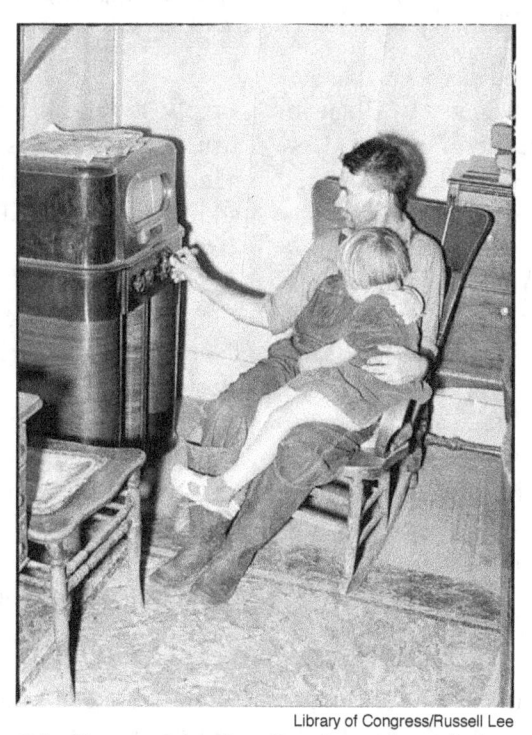

Library of Congress/Russell Lee

John Front and daughter listening to the radio in their home.

A Dialogue with the American People

On March 12, 1933, only eight days after taking office, Franklin Roosevelt addressed the American people, by radio, in the first of what would become known as his "Fireside Chats." During those eight days, FDR had taken a series of bold emergency actions to deal with the national banking and financial crisis, including the passage of the Emergency Banking Act on March 9 and the declaration of a four-day "bank holiday." At that time, sixty percent of American households owned radios, and on March 12, FDR became the first President to speak directly to the majority of the American people. He began by saying,

I want to talk for a few minutes with the people of the United States about banking—with the comparatively few who understand the mechanics of banking but more particularly with the overwhelming majority who use banks for the making of deposits and the drawing of checks. I want to tell you what has been done in the last few days, why it was done, and what the next steps are going to be...

Roosevelt gave a concise presentation on how banking worked, why a national bank holiday had been necessary, and the actual state of the banking system in the United States at that time. The affect on the American people was powerful and almost immediate.

Over the course of his

twelve-year presidency, Roosevelt delivered thirty Fireside Chats. In response, millions of letters flooded the White House. Farmers, business owners, men, women, rich, poor—most of them expressed the feeling that the President had entered their home and spoken directly to them. This was not a one-way street in which FDR simply "reported" to the American people. It was a dialogue, wherein the American people were recruited into active participation in a discussion process as to merits of crucial policy initiatives and the future course of the nation.

VI. What Is Needed Today

It is extremely illuminating to read and study the dozens of speeches which President Franklin Roosevelt delivered during both his first 100 Days, and throughout the entirety of his first year in office. Many issues are discussed. His initiatives to deal with the banking crisis particularly dominate many of his initial addresses. Yet, throughout that three to twelve month period, one theme drowns out all the others. Put people back to work! Again, and again, and again, FDR hammers away at the absolute necessity for aggressive action to provide citizens with useful, gainful, employment.

Recently, a great deal of attention has been given to the seemingly miraculous accomplishment by China in uplifting 700 million of its people out of poverty. Unfortunately, most of the news media deal with this breakthrough as if it were a "statistic." "Lifting people out of poverty" is not a statistic; it is not about numbers. The accomplishment is one of uplifting hundreds of millions out of despair and degradation into an environment of hope and optimism. This is the necessary pre-condition for the emergence of a Renaissance within human society. What will have an even more profound impact, is if the new jobs that are created are ones that do not simply provide income, but are also producing tangible, visible improvements within society as a whole. Thus, the culture of the entire nation is uplifted. A sense of mission takes hold. A dynamic leading to a profound increase in national productivity is unleashed.

According to the 2009 "Infrastructure Report Card," issued by the American Society of Civil Engineers, America now needs to spend $1.13 trillion

Library of Congress

Rural electrification, one of FDR's major initiatives, in California's San Joaquin Valley in 1938.

simply to sustain and repair already existing infrastructure (e.g., roads, bridges, dams, levees) within the nation. The report also states that it would require an additional $4.69 trillion to build the absolutely necessary new infrastructure required to meet the nation's needs over the next two decades. That's a total of almost six trillion dollars. During his campaign, President-elect Donald Trump, to his credit, repeatedly stated his intention to spend $1 trillion on the nation's infrastructure. Despite the fact that this would be the strongest commitment by any U.S. President to such an effort since the assassination of John Kennedy, it is still far too little.

The Civil Engineers' report includes only such future projects as they deem "necessary." It does not include a national high-speed rail system, Fusion Energy research, NASA funding, a Bering Strait tunnel to connect to the Eurasian Landbridge, a bold fresh water development program, or other such projects. It includes nothing on the scale of FDR's Tennessee

Valley Authority. So their figure of $4.69 trillion for new infrastructure construction is far too small.

Between 1933 and 1935 the Federal Emergency Relief Administration (the forerunner of the WPA) and the Public Works Administration together spent $9.1 billion on infrastructure construction. That represented 12.5 percent of the nation's Gross Domestic Product (GDP). An equivalent expenditure for today's GDP would be $2.3 trillion. And that $9.1 billion figure was only what was spent by FERA and the PWA; it does not include any of the additional spending by the TVA, the CCC, the NYA or several other agencies active in the first years of the New Deal. It also does not include the credit made available through the Reconstruction Finance Corporation or the reorganized commercial banking system.

It is also a certainty that, were a full "Roosevelt approach" taken today, this would result in the creation of, minimally, twenty to thirty million new, productive jobs.

Saving the Citizenry for 'That which is Better'

On March 6, 1936 Franklin Roosevelt delivered his Annual Address to the United States Congress. In it, he stated,

In March, 1933, the problems which faced our Nation and which only our national Government had the resources to meet were more serious even than appeared on the surface.

It was not only that the visible mechanism of economic life had broken down. More disturbing was the fact that long neglect of the needs of the underprivileged had brought too many of our people to the verge of doubt as to the successful adaptation of our historic traditions to the complex modern world. In that lay a challenge to our democratic form of Government itself...

Ours was the task to do more than to argue a theory. The times required the confident answer of performance to those whose instinctive faith in humanity made them want to believe that in the long run democracy would prove superior to more extreme forms of Government as a process of getting action when action was wisdom, without the spiritual sacrifices which those other forms of Government exact.

That challenge we met. To meet it required

unprecedented activities under Federal leadership to end abuses, to restore a large measure of material prosperity, to give new faith to millions of our citizens who had been traditionally taught to expect that democracy would provide continuously wider opportunity and continuously greater security in a world where science was continuously making material riches more available to man...

Nor was the recovery we sought merely a purposeless whirring of machinery. It is important, of course, that every man and woman in the country be able to find work, that every factory run, that business and farming as a whole earn profits. But Government in a democratic Nation does not exist solely, or even primarily, for that purpose.

It is not enough that the wheels turn. They must carry us in the direction of a greater satisfaction in life for the average man. The deeper purpose of democratic government is to assist as many of its citizens as possible, especially those who need it most, to improve their conditions of life, to retain all personal liberty which does not adversely affect their neighbors, and to pursue the happiness which comes with security and an opportunity for recreation and culture.

Even with our present recovery we are far from the goal of that deeper purpose. There are far-reaching problems still with us for which democracy must find solutions if it is to consider itself successful.

It is useful to note, that during the period of 1933 to 1935, while the fascist regimes of Hitler and Mussolini enforced their dictatorships through the deployment of "blackshirts," "brownshirts," and other murderous "fascisti" composed largely of previously unemployed and displaced youth, a similar problem never arose in the United States. There was, indeed, a powerful *bona fide* fascist element, led by groups such as Jacob Raskob's American Liberty League, the Crusaders, the Black Legion and the American Bund—almost all of whom had deep ties to Wall Street—but there was no fascist mass movement of American youth. Instead, those youth were in Roosevelt's CCC camps, or employed through the NYA, or working on a CWA project, or receiving music training through the Federal Music

Project. This is what is possible when despair is transformed to hope.

VII. Granting Access to the Sublime

In addition to the "jobs program" presented above, there exists, today, an even more powerful weapon available to our movement in this crusade to rescue our nation. An inkling as to the nature of that weapon is to be found in the activities of the Schiller Institute New York Community Chorus over the past twenty-four months.

On the one hand, the multiple performances of Handel's *Messiah,* African-American spirituals and other classical compositions throughout the New York metropolitan area, particularly the "Living Memorial" concerts on the fifteenth anniversary of the 9/11 attacks, has effected a powerful intervention into a population dragged down by pessimism and fear over the last fifteen years. The concerts and related activities have been a living "clarion call" to all New Yorkers to find "that which is better" within each of us.

The potential of this embryonic process is still much greater. Earlier, in this article, material was presented as to the state of youth in present-day America. It is a generation saturated with both legal and illegal drugs, one in which the ability to carry out sustained, concentrated creative work has been severely damaged, and one in which the experience of true human optimism is almost unknown. How does one go about changing this?

The classical approach of the Schiller Institute Chorus, under its leaders, provides the correct pathway. Participants in such a chorus are involved in sustained work, sustained concentration, all of which is intended to produce something beautiful, something universally true. There is an obvious moral component in this, but there is also the neurological issue. Let us be very explicit here. Marijuana use is now epidemic among young people, and regular use of marijuana impairs cognitive functioning. The video game/social media culture furthers this cognitive destruction. The mind loses its higher capacities and the soul is enervated. The choral principal, as now underway in New York, pro-

EIRNS/Stuart Lewis

Members of the Schiller Institute Chorus rehearse under the leadership of Diane Sare.

vides "creative therapy," in a manner of speaking, to strengthen the human identity. New cognitive powers, language skills, ear-training and concentration skills are being developed.

Imagine a very young girl who is given a violin and provided with a good teacher. As the child works with her instrument over a period of weeks and months, an entire new world opens up. New levels of human understanding, previously completely unknown, emerge; new powers of cognition; a greater understanding of artistic beauty. Glimpses of what Friedrich Schiller identified as "The Sublime" begin to take hold within the mind and heart of the young violinist.[4] An unseen, but sensed, higher identity, one which is both beautiful and lawful, offers itself to the young artist.

Essentially, what is being discussed here is the creation of a new Cultural Platform for America, which is, in fact, absolutely indispensable for the rescuing of the American people.

Everything that must be done over the coming period—economically, financially, artistically, morally—must be governed by a principle of upward progress, progress which is visible—tangible—as an active idea within society. In this way America can be rescued and become, once again, an active friend and partner to other nations throughout the world.

---

4. In her autobiography, Marian Anderson describes how she bought her first violin, for $3.98, from a pawnshop when she was nine years old.

Every Day Counts In Today's Showdown To Save Civilization

That's why you need EIR's **Daily Alert Service**, a strategic overview compiled with the input of Lyndon LaRouche, and delivered to your email 5 days a week.

The election of Donald Trump to the Presidency of the Untied States has launched a new global era whose character has yet to be determined. The Obama-Clinton drive toward confrontation with Russia has been disrupted--but what will come next?

Over the next weeks and months there will be a pitched battle to determine the course of the Trump Administration. Will it pursue policies of cooperation with Russia and China in the New Silk Road, as the President-Elect has given some signs of? Will it follow through against Wall Street with Glass-Steagall?

The opposition to these policies will be fierce. If there is to be a positive outcome to this battle, an informed citizenry must do its part--intervening, educating, inspiring. That's why you need the EIR Daily Alert more than ever.

TUESDAY, NOVEMBER 22, 2016

Volume 3, Number 65

EIR Daily Alert Service

P.O. Box 17390, Washington, DC 20041-0390

- Only Global Solutions, Based on New Principles, Can Work
- Tulsi Gabbard Meets with Donald Trump Regarding Syria
- Robert Kagan Throws in the Towel, Complains U.S. Is Becoming 'Solipsistic'
- War Party Moving To Preempt Trump-Putin Reset
- Syrian Army Makes More Progress in Aleppo
- Duterte Gives OK to Nuclear Power for Philippines
- Europe Will Suffer from Maintaining Russia Sanctions
- Former Chilean Diplomat Confirmed, 'We Will Joyfully Welcome Xi Jinping'
- Duterte and Putin Establish Philippines-Russia Cooperation
- François Fillon, Pro-Russian Thatcherite, Wins First Round of French Right-Wing Presidential Primary

EDITORIAL

Only Global Solutions, Based on New Principles, Can Work

II. Word from Africa

Transaqua: A Dream Is Becoming Reality

By Claudio Celani

Dec. 31—Over the past two years, this author has had the privilege of participating in high-level discussions and negotiations to build the largest infrastructural project Africa has ever seen, called "Transaqua." As a result of this effort, on December 13, 2016, a Memorandum of Understanding was signed in Abuja, Nigeria, between the Lake Chad Basin Commission (LCBC) and the Chinese engineering and construction firm PowerChina, for a feasibility study and eventually the construction of the project.

"Transaqua" is an idea developed by the Italian engineering firm Bonifica in the late 1970s. A team led by Dr. Marcello Vichi drafted a proposal on how to solve the Sahel crisis, provoked by the progressive drying out of Lake Chad, which was already producing an increasing flow of refugees into Europe. Vichi's team came up with the idea of a waterway which would be able to replenish the lake, and at the same time form a giant transport, energy and agricultural infrastructure for Central Africa. The construction of such an infrastructure project would offer jobs for millions of Africans, and lay the basis for future development.

Simple and Ingenious

The idea of Transaqua is both simple and ingenious at the same time.

It has been undisputed that unless Lake Chad begins receiving a major transfer of fresh water, the lake will die, jeopardizing the lives of 30-plus million people who live on its shore. It has also been clear that this water should come from the Congo basin, which is separated from the Chad basin by a mountain chain, running along the border between Chad and the Central African Republic (CAR).

The Congo basin, in fact, has plenty of water. The Congo River is the second largest river in the world, with an average discharge of 41,000 cubic meters per second, which flows unused into the ocean. The Bonifica team calculated that 3-4% of that water would be enough to replenish Lake Chad.

The problem to be solved was that to bring water

EIR

Left to right: Mohammed Bila (LCBC), Andrea Mangano, Marcello Vichi, and the author, discussing plans for Transaqua in the Rome Bonifica office, summer 2015.

directly from the Congo River to the Chad basin, it must be carried uphill. A canal is unthinkable, and to pump the water through pipelines is an effort of gigantic costs, in terms of energy and dimensions.

A Brilliant Solution

The Bonifica team came up with a brilliant solution: instead of taking water directly from the Congo River, take it from its west bank tributaries at high altitude, starting in the southern region of the Democratic Republic of Congo (DRC) and reaching, by means of gravity, the CAR-Chad watershed. There, at an elevation of about 500 meters, the water would be channeled into the Chari River, a tributary of Lake Chad.

In this way, a 2,400 km-long waterway could be built, crossing all west bank tributaries of the Congo River where dams and water reservoirs would be built. As a result, up to 100 billion cubic meters of water per annum could be collected and poured into Lake Chad. It was calculated that half of that amount would be enough to replenish the lake, and the rest would be available for irrigation of an area as large as two times the lake itself.

Moreover, the water reservoirs and the dams built on each and every tributary would regulate the river flows, allowing agricultural extensions and generation of electricity. And, by not taking the water all at once from one river, but in small amounts from each tributary, there would be practically no impact on navigability and fishing of the rivers.

The waterway itself would be a navigable infrastructure, 100 meters wide and 10 meters deep, stretching from south DRC to the northern border of the CAR. The waterway would be flanked by a service road (necessary for the construction) or, eventually, a rail-

way. In the CAR itself, a larger water reservoir would be built.

Lyndon LaRouche Sees the Potential

When the Transaqua idea was presented to Lyndon LaRouche in the early 1990s, he immediately recognized the potential for a productive platform that would change the face of Africa. He made Transaqua part of his international campaign for development.

Meanwhile IRI, the state conglomerate of which the Italian firm Bonifica was a part, was privatized as part of the Euro agreements, before even a feasibility study of Transaqua could be done. Dr. Vichi, however, never ceased his battle for Transaqua, and set up a website

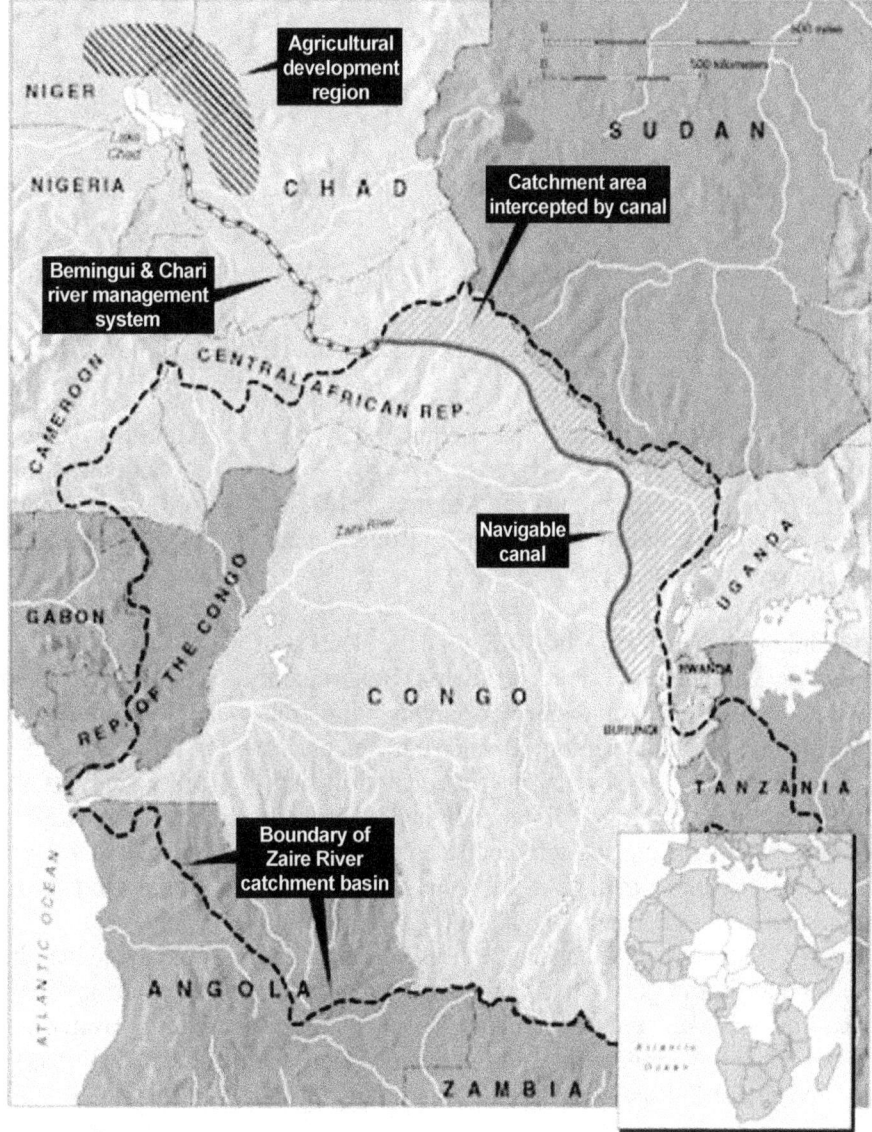

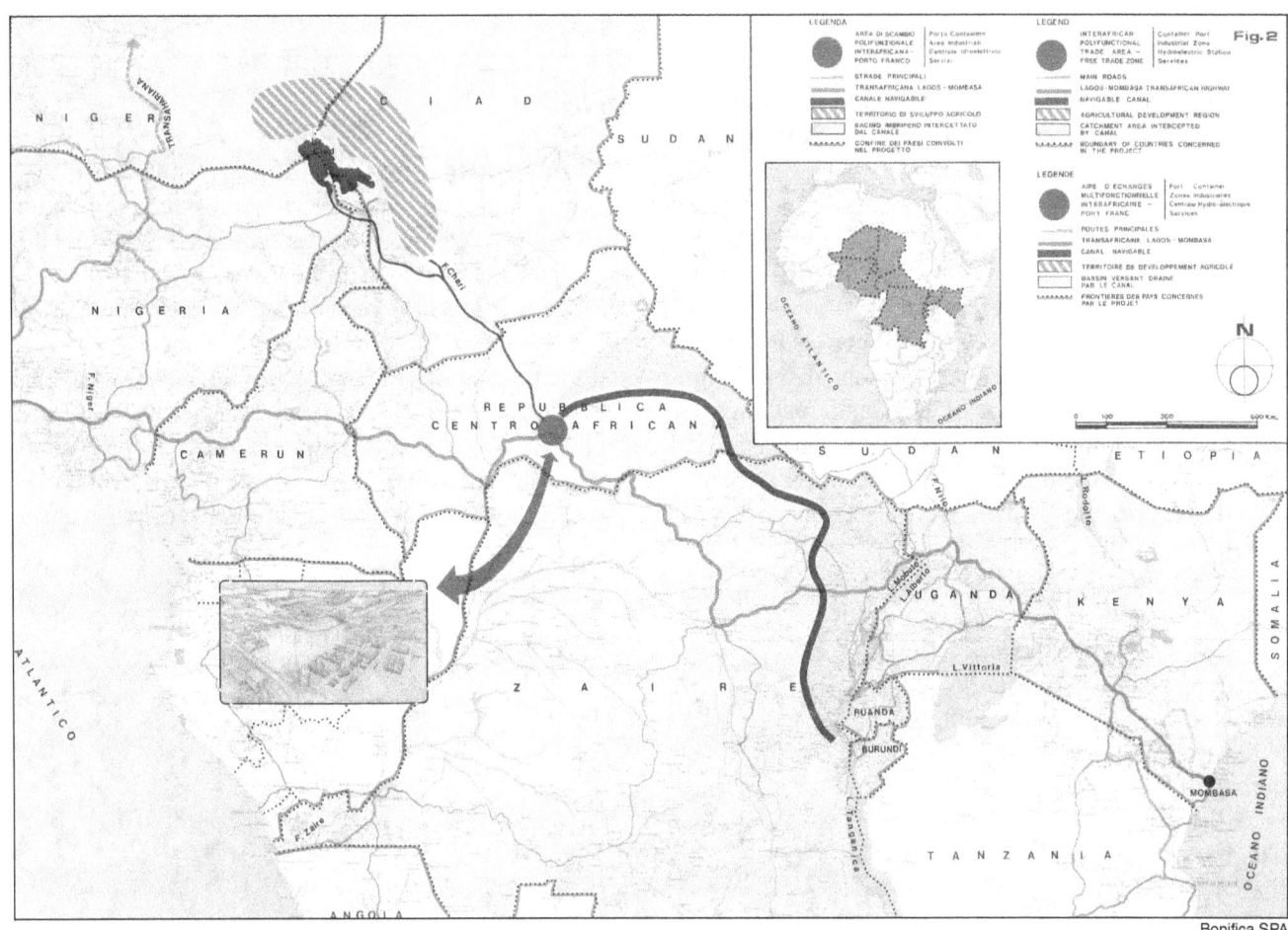

Bonifica SPA

where all of its records have been compiled (http://www.transaquaproject.it/).

Later on, Dr. Vichi and his collaborator, Dr. Andrea Mangano, joined efforts with the LaRouche campaign (see for instance http://www.larouchepub.com/pr/2016/160322_frankfurt_seminar.html)

The shift occurred in May 2015, with the election of President Muhammad Buhari in Nigeria. Buhari came to power with a program to develop national infrastructure, including implementing a water-transfer project for Lake Chad. On several international occasions, Buhari has made a strong point for solving the problem of Lake Chad, asking Western countries to deliver on promises for financial aid. At the same time, the new government has engaged in an all-out fight against the terrorist Boko Haram, which has been recruiting among poor youth in the Lake Chad region, and even had its bases on the lake. President Buhari has also strongly oriented his government towards cooperation with the BRICS (Brazil, Russia, India, China, South Africa) countries.

Nigeria's Role

Nigeria has historically been the leader, with respect to the Lake Chad issue, of the five most affected countries (Camerooon, Chad, Niger, Nigeria, and CAR), which form the LCBC. The Commission Executive Secretary, Eng. Abdullahi Sanusi Imran, is also political coordinator of the International Coalition which, under Nigerian military leadership, has been fighting Boko Haram.

Mr. Sanusi's predecessor had commissioned a feasibility study of a water-transfer project for Lake Chad, but for mysterious reasons, instead of adopting Transaqua, focused on the idea of taking water from one single tributary of the Congo River, the Oubangi. The study, made by the Canadian engineering firm CIMA, concluded that the project was technically feasible, but it would involve a giant effort in terms of costs and energy (water must be pumped uphill for several hundred kilometers) and ultimately, the amount of water would not be sufficient to replenish Lake Chad.

To reach this conclusion, which was evident from the

beginning, given the limited discharge of the Oubangi River, the Canadians presented a bill of $5 million.

EIR Involved

In 2015 the LCBC provided the CIMA study to *EIR*, which, through assistance from Dr. Vichi and his colleague, Andrea Mangano, was able to persuade the LCBC to drop the Oubangi idea as insane, and to finally adopt Transaqua.

After an event in N'Djamena, Chad, in November 2014, where *EIR* had presented the Transaqua idea to the LCBC, *EIR* organized a first contact between the LCBC and the Transaqua authors in Rome, in the Bonifica offices, on Sept. 5, 2015. As a result of that meeting, a few weeks later the LCBC sent a request to Bonifica for a pre-feasibility study of the Transaqua idea.

Details of the offer were eventually discussed in Paris, in December of the same year, among Vichi, Mangano and the LCBC Executive Secretary. It was decided that, in order to begin the project as soon as possible, a study should be conducted to determine how much water could be transferred by building the CAR tract of Transaqua. This, because the Democratic Republic of Congo was not yet on board, or worse, a probably foreign-steered campaign against Transaqua had come from Congo circles in the recent years, using the argument that Transaqua would "steal the Congo's water." This argument was silly, especially because Congo would be a net beneficiary of the project by acquiring a navigable waterway, electricity production, and regulation of rivers.

The Transaqua authors accepted Mr. Sanusi's proposal, on the condition that the feasibility study should involve the entire project, so that once the CAR tract is built, the rest of Transaqua could be built just by extension.

After some weeks, the offer was delivered, including detailed Terms of Reference and methodology. Mr. Sanusi acknowledged, in a communication to the Italians, that "the Transaqua concept is much more appropriate for the situation of the Lake Chad" than all other solutions.

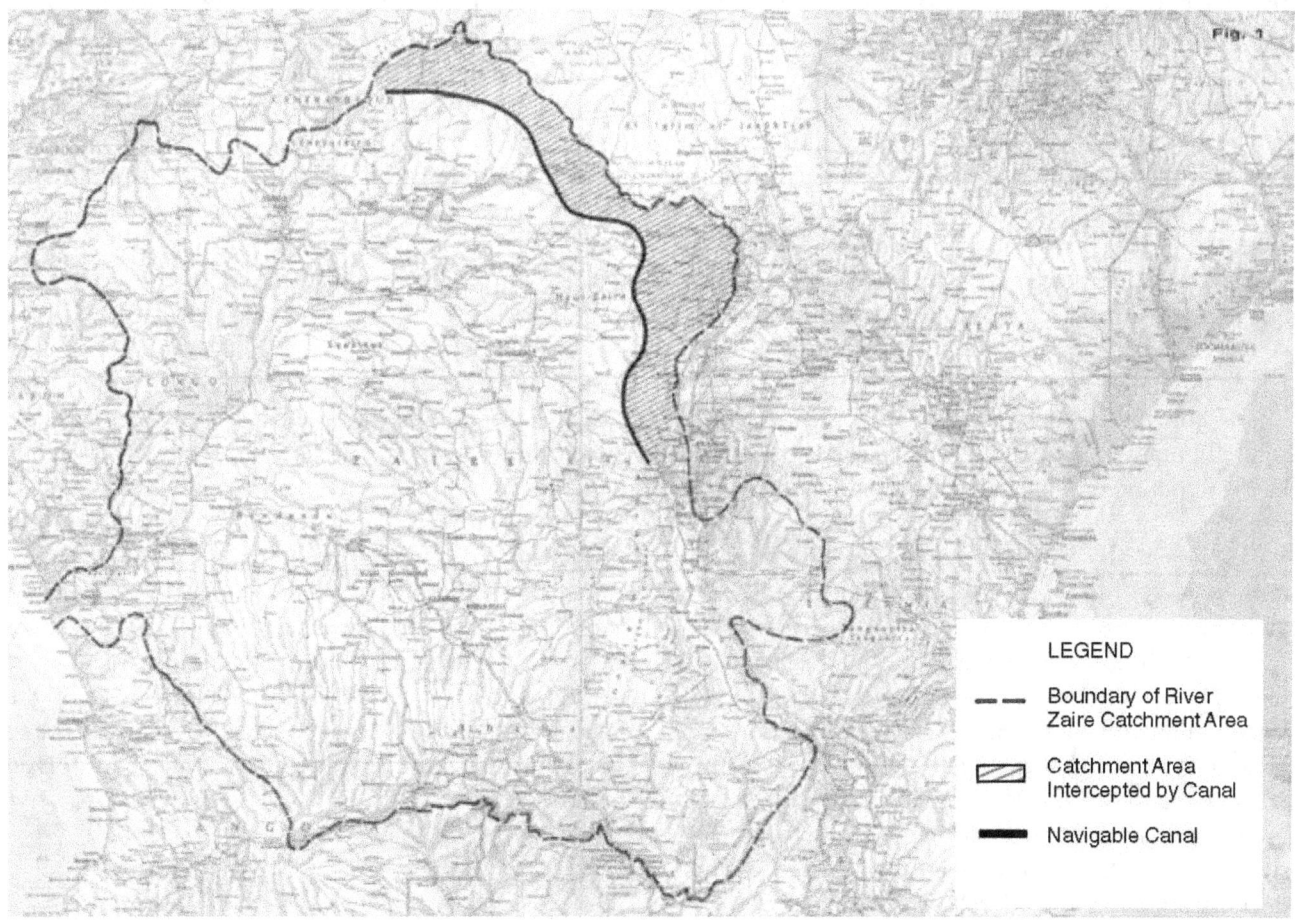

LEGEND

– – – Boundary of River
Zaire Catchment Area

▨ Catchment Area
Intercepted by Canal

▬ Navigable Canal

Nigerian Crisis

In the meantime, however, the economic situation of Nigeria had dramatically changed and a major financial crisis had erupted. Due to the fall of oil prices, foreign revenues had dramatically collapsed, and Nigeria began to have a negative balance of payments. Furthermore, a new terrorist group, called "The avengers of the Niger Delta," popped up out of nowhere, sabotaging pipelines and causing a reduction of up to 30% of national oil production.

Additionally, international financial circles pressured Nigeria to devalue its currency. President Buhari resisted for months, as he knew that if he did so, this would provoke a major increase of, mostly, imported food prices. Ultimately, he backed down in May 2016, and the situation has been deteriorating ever since. The military campaign against Boko Haram has been scoring major successes, but also draining resources. Nigeria must borrow money from abroad.

New Silk Road to Lake Chad

In this situation, the LCBC solved the problem by bringing the New Silk Road to Lake Chad! PowerChina, one of the largest Chinese multinationals and the company that built the Three Gorges Dam, signed a Memorandum of Understanding with the LCBC on Dec. 13, in which PowerChina commits to finance the feasibility study for the initial stages of Transaqua, as discussed with its authors, and eventually to build the infrastructure.

PowerChina, the report states, will study the feasibility of "an African Infrastructure project by opening a new corridor of development linking West and Central Africa through:

"1. Potentially transferring 50 billion cubic meters annually to the Lake Chad through a series of dams in DRC, Republic of Congo and the Central African Republic.

"2. Potentially generating up to 15 to 25 thousand million kWh of hydroelectricity through the mass movement of the water by gravity.

"3. Potentially developing a series of irrigated areas for crops, or livestock over an area of 50,000 to 70,000 square kilometers in the Sahel zone in Chad, northeast Nigeria, northern Cameroon and Niger.

"4. Creating an expanded economic zone by providing a new infrastructure platform of development in agriculture, industries, transportation, and electrical production, affecting up to 12 African nations.

"The core idea," the statement continues, "is to increase the water quantity in Lake Chad, to improve the water flow conditions, to alleviate poverty within the basin through socio-economic activities, to meet the energy needs of towns … surrounding … the … Congo and to conduct an in-depth environmental impact assessment."[1]

In remarks at the signing, reported by Nigerian media, "the Vice-President of PowerChina, Mr. Tian Hailua, said that the company was committing both technical and financial assistance towards the actualization of the water transfer to the lake. He added that the company has agreed to fund the project to the tune of U.S. $1.8 million in order to make life more meaningful, socially and economically, to the people within the basin. He explained that, with the transfer of water to the lake, there is the potential to develop a series of irrigated areas for crops and livestock of over 50,000 to 70,000 square kilometers in the basin."

Nigeria Water Minister Suleiman Adamu "noted that the project is a generational project, as it would take a long time to actualize due to the huge capital involved and the complexity of the nature the project." He called for "concerted efforts from all to see that the project is achievable, as this would save the livelihood of over 40 million people living within the basin."

Although the volume of water-transfer specified is half the volume of the original Transaqua project, it will be enough to refill Lake Chad. However, it is expected that the PowerChina study will explore the feasibility of building a system of dams and waterways which can be extended southwards in the Democratic Republic of Congo, involving all of the right-side tributaries of the Congo River. In this way, the project will not only be a simple water transfer, but also a major transport infrastructure connecting all nations of central Africa.

"To be complete, the feasibility study should explore, from the beginning, the complete length of the water-transfer project," Transaqua author Marcello Vichi stated, "even if the canal, obviously, should necessarily start from the North, in Central African territory, to proceed southwards as much as allowed by the available funds and by national will. The longer the canal, the bigger will be the water volume to be poured into the lake."

1. http://www.cblt.org/en/news/inter-basin-water-transfer-project-signing-memorandum-understanding-between-lcbc-and-PowerChina

Africa Urgently Needs America To Be Great Again

A New Year's Message to President-Elect Trump

I am Ramasimong Phillip Tsokolibane, the spokesperson for the LaRouche movement here in the Republic of South Africa. In my greeting to you, President-elect Donald J. Trump, and to the American people, I believe I am expressing the hopes of my fellow South African citizens, and of all Africans, for your success.

Mr. Trump: You are coming into office riding an international wave of popular opposition to, and rejection of, the powerful elite which has run the collapsing trans-Atlantic financial empire and its failed policies, which have left most of the world, including much of your nation, in economic ruin. Two terms of misdirection by President Barack Obama have brought America to the brink of military confrontation and possible thermonuclear war with Russia and China, which no sane person desires. Obama has launched regime-change wars and has supported and armed terrorists, murdering populations at a genocidal rate around the globe. I can tell you frankly that the United States of Barack Obama, his clone (and your defeated opponent) Hillary Clinton, and the Bushes, whose policies Obama copies, is reviled around the globe and here in Africa, and he is supported only by the flunkies of the dying Anglo-American empire.

But coming from the East, at the direction of Presidents Putin in Russia and Xi of China, are important initiatives which, if properly understood and joined by yourself and the American people, can reverse the curse of Obama, who is really no more than a puppet of the evil British Queen and her oligarchical retinue.

Ramasimong Phillip Tsokolibane

We now have an opportunity to literally build a new future for all of mankind—one that can rapidly lead to a new era of cooperation among nations—ending the geopolitics and competition that pit peoples and nations against each other for the benefit of the degenerate monetarists and their empire of money. We must make all mankind rich in a future of creative discoveries, of breakthroughs in science that will drive civilization as a whole towards leaps in progress.

Such a world, until recently, could only be dreamed of by great men, such as your own Martin Luther King, Jr., and our father, Nelson Mandela, but which Wall Street and the City of London conspired to crush.

The creation of the BRICS alliance, of which my nation is a proud member, with its commitment to deploy massive amounts of credit for what is called large-scale 'infrastructure' development, as in China's 'One Belt, One Road' policy, is the seed crystal for a new global system, one that ends the enforced under-development in Africa and elsewhere. This policy is wholly American in its origin and is based on the American System of physical economy, as designed by your first Treasury Secretary, the great Alexander Hamilton (see his Four Reports to Congress); he understood that all value is generated by the continuous improvement in human productive labor. It has been the explicit policy of the leading modern advocate of Hamilton's system, the statesman Lyndon LaRouche, world's leading physical economist.

LaRouche's 'update' of Hamilton, as laid out in his 'Four Laws',[1] rejects the monetarist system's treatment of men as beasts, as a herd that is to be culled by a self-appointed elite, and instead makes the continuous realization of Man's creative potential the principal force in the universe for change for the good. Government—all governments—must act from the principle which is the linchpin of your own Constitution: that all policy must serve the General Welfare, by acting now to improve the future condition of all people, not just some decadent oligarchical elite.

What is actually being proposed by the Chinese and the Russians is a policy of mutual benefit and improvement which serves the principle of the General Welfare, whose modern advocacy can be traced directly to the work of Mr. LaRouche and his wife, the 'Silk Road Lady', Helga Zepp-LaRouche, over the last 50 years. As I said, this is really an 'American' policy, in the tradition of Hamilton, Henry Carey, Abraham Lincoln, and in the last century, Franklin Roosevelt and John Kennedy.

It is truly not only in America's real interest, but it is also its historic mission, as bequeathed by Hamilton and your Founding Fathers, to lead the world revolution against British monetarism and its beastman policies, the which must invariably lead to population collapse, because such an anti-human economy can never support and sustain even existing population levels, especially under conditions of financial collapse. Today, unless such policies are reversed, Africa faces a deliberate and predictable genocide on a scale that would make the British-initiated golem, Adolf Hitler, blush with envy. We, in Africa, look at the new initiatives coming from fellow BRICS members Russia and China, for nuclear energy deployment and other infra-structure, as not merely desirable, but essential for our survival.

But, if we are to find our way to a future of peace and progress, we must reach out to you, Mr. Trump and to your great American republic, and ask that you, too, help lift us away from the beckoning abyss. We Africans do not beg. We simply ask that you resume the true mantle of greatness for which your nation was created, in revolution against the servitude of British imperialism. Let America join with the world's other great continental powers, Russia and China, in placing human creative development at the center of a new era of peace and development, and we will have both.

In the 1980s, when he ran for President of your nation, Mr. LaRouche offered a televised message that depicted a future Earth colony on Mars led by an American woman scientist. This expression of a mission for mankind was crushed by the successive Bush governments and the government of the Bush clone, Obama, that have destroyed your manned space program. But the time has come to once again dream great dreams, and to place Man outside and off of this small planet, and into the universe in search of new discoveries and knowledge. It is my hope that, with the help of the American people, the 'Woman on Mars' might be African!

In offering our hand in friendship, we Africans understand—especially in this time of year when we reflect on our humanity and the essential goodness of mankind—that your help for us and others in need in the world, also helps your own nation, not only in a partnership for economic development, but on the spiritual plane, as we all become better human beings. It is, therefore, in the spirit of the ecumenism of this season that we seek true 'peace on Earth and goodwill towards all men and women' everywhere.

So, I greet the American people and remind them that the world needs you to become the great people that Hamilton, Lincoln, Franklin Roosevelt, and Kennedy urged you to be. And to you, President-elect Trump, I extend the hand of friendship from Africa, and wish you success in your oft-stated goal of making America the great nation that it was intended to be and must be, once again.

Ramasimong Phillip Tsokolibane
23 December 2016

---

1. http://larouchepub.com/eiw/public/2016/
eirv43n46-20161111/06-11_4346.pdf